SSH... IT HAPPENED AGAIN!

MORE RURAL RHYMES

First Published in Great Britain 2016 by Mirador Publishing

First edition: 2016

Any reference to real names and places are purely fictional and are constructs of the author. Any offence the references produce is unintentional and in no way reflects the reality of any locations or people involved.

A copy of this work is available through the British Library.

ISBN: 978-1-911473-46-6

Mirador Publishing
Mirador
Wearne Lane
Langport
Somerset
TA10 9HB

Ssh..It Happened Again!
More Rural Rhymes.

By

Jan Millward

Introduction

This is my second little book of rural rhymes and I have had so much fun putting it together.

I was encouraged to go ahead with this book by the massive support I have had on farming forums on the internet and also by the fantastic feedback from family and friends who have "been there, done that"!

Working on a farm can be a very solitary role these days and if I can make a few of you have a chuckle or have a wry smile then my job here is done!

British Farmers.

Our stunning British countryside,
the rolling hills and vales.
The woodlands and the orchards,
the soaring peaks and dales.

The patchwork fields of England,
the bleakness of the moors.
The flower farms in Cornwall,
these views are mine and yours.

The sweeping Brecon Beacons,
the valleys and the sea.
Snowdonia's mighty mountains,
are there for all to see.

The cider apple orchards,
the vales of fruit and flowers.
The footpaths and the country lanes,
where we can roam for hours.

The peaks and lakes and pathways,
the Scottish lochs and glens.
The wild offshore islands,
the flatness of the fens.

The emerald green of Ireland,
Our North, South, East and West.
The stunning coastal pathways,
we truly have the best.

Our farmers are the guardians,
of our green and pleasant land,
they work the fields and pastures,
and their future's in our hands.

Baler twine has been used for generations as the universal "go to" for emergency repairs.

Farmers friend.

If the gate has come off its hinges,
or the bull has escaped from the pen.
If the mud guards come loose on the tractor,
or you need to transport a hen.

If your trousers are losing elastic,
or the horse won't move through the gate.
When you really need proper fencing,
but already are running quite late.

If the bottom falls out of your barrow,
or you need to tie up a calf.
When the sheep have broken some netting,
or you need to block off the footpath.

The one thing all farmers rely on,
for emergency use great and small,
is a pocketful of baler twine,
rolled up in a neat little ball.

Farming isn't always as it is portrayed on the television, with knowledgeable presenters waxing lyrical about the farmer.
Most of us will have done some of these jobs and messed up just as badly as I have on occasions!

No one is perfect.

I have been an egg collector
covered in thick grey dust,
stacking eggs on trolleys
just to earn a crust.

I have been a chicken plucker
in barns covered in snow,
with feathers in my eyebrows
just to earn some dough.

I have picked and sorted 'taters
and weeded rows of beet.
I have rogued wild oats in corn fields,
whilst sweating in the heat.

I have dug out heaving maggots
from the flesh of poor old ewes.
It's not a job to cherish
or one that most would choose.

I have tagged a thousand cattle
and pared a million feet,
I have stripped out stringy udders
and dropped hammers on my feet.

I have fallen in the slurry
and been knocked out by a cow.
I have burnt my hand whilst welding,
and been chased by an old sow.

I have run out of my wellies
when I got stuck in mud.
I have driven through a river
to reach heifers in a flood.

I have stuck myself with needles
and injected my own thigh,
but I've just had to carry on
and hoped that I didn't die.

I've been covered in the mucus
from a calf I had to pull.
I was just a little worried
when I got cornered by the bull.

I have fallen off a trailer
and got the tractor stuck,
and when I wasn't looking
a cow covered me in muck.

When you see them on the tele'
and they're showing off in style,
you think that isn't farming
and you have to have a smile.

Show me a real farmer
who really knows the score
who isn't always perfect,
then I might watch some more!

Almond milk is very popular these days and is a very useful alternative to cow's milk for those who are lactose-intolerant. This poem is a tongue in cheek look at how exactly an almond is milked.

The nutty farmer.

I've had enough of milking cows all of the day.
I'm sick of spending weekends out there making hay.
I'm done with getting smelly with cow muck on my clothes,
I've had enough of washing yards down with a hose.

I've had my fill of calving in fields out on my own.
I'm fed up with the bank saying I can't have a loan.
I can't waste one more minute on milk that doesn't pay,
I'm looking for an answer, I'll try another way.

I'm told that there is money to be made by milking nuts.
Some trendy folk like almonds to flavour tea in cups.
I'm not sure how to do it, I don't like climbing trees,
but I'll find a way around it, I'll do my best to please.

I have to ask some questions, like "Do you squeeze them tight"?
"How often do you milk them? Morning, noon or night"?
Almonds are more often used when they are ground,
or toasted on a cake until they're nice and golden brown.

I need to find a farmer who has milked nuts all his life.
I want to ask him truly if he drinks it with his wife?
How does he get the units to hang on to the nuts?
I want to do it properly, I don't want ifs or buts.

So if you grew up squeezing milk out from a nut,
it might have been an almond, brazil or hazelnut.
Can you please write to me and tell me how it's done,
I could make lots of money, and it might just be great fun!

I love my chickens and as a child I would spend hours sat out in the field with them, learning their behaviour. I still find the hatching process magical, even after all these years!

The chicken whisperer.

I am a chicken whisperer, my friends think I'm quite mad.
But they don't know the half of it, I think it's rather sad.
I grew up in the country, my friends were hens and ducks.
I spent so many hours with them they taught me how to cluck!

I'd always be surrounded by Marans and White Leghorns,
with pockets full of marbles, string and flakes of corn.
I knew when they were happy or getting in a fluster,
I knew when they were laying brown eggs in a cluster.

I had multi coloured bantie's with feathers on their feet.
We spent so long together, I understood each tweet.
I'd be the first to go out and open all their pens,
It was when I was quite little that I knew that I loved hens.

I giggled when the broody got cross and pecked Dads hand.
My friends all came to see them but they didn't understand.
I spent my life protecting young chicks from crows and rooks,
I found out all about them from my Dad and farming books.

And then there was the heartache when the fox killed all but three.
I thought I'd cry forever, when I saw his killing spree.
I love to see the mother hens with chicks under their wings,
and seeing little heads poke out, is such a powerful thing.

I like to see hens scratching and bathing in the dust,
picking over scraps of food, peelings and a crust.
And then you are rewarded with eggs with golden yolks.
If you're a chicken whisperer, you're not like other folk!

People may come and go, they will let you down and hurt you.
But your dog will always be there for you whatever is happening
in your life.

Your dog.

When you don't know what's in store,
and you can't take life any more.
When you feel you have no hope,
when you think you cannot cope.

When life is hard and you feel beat.
When you are worn out on your feet.
When you have given all you've got,
and you have nearly lost the plot.

Look at your dog, into his eyes,
he will not tell you any lies.
He will be faithful, always there,
when you are feeling in despair.

A dog will be your true best friend,
he'll stay by you until his end.
He'll never falter or give in,
he'll be your friend through thick and thin.

Call out his name and see him run
into your arms, your heart he's won.
Give him a hug and you will find,
so many worries left behind.

A dog will know if you feel rough,
if you have taken quite enough.
He'll offer you a love that's pure,
much better than a doctors cure.

A dog is more than just a pet,
he'll comfort you when you're upset.
He'll bring you joy that never fails,
with friendly licks and wags of tails.

Smell has the power to bring memories flooding back. The smell of sweet well made hay has got to be up there as one of my favourite farm smells!

The sweet smell of hay.

The smell of sweet hay can release a storehouse of memories.
Hot, cloudless days, the beat of the baler
scooping up trails of sun dried grass and churning it out
in neat oblong packages.
The relentless sun, baking the wilted stems,
freeing the glorious scent to drift carelessly into the soul.
Sweat on tanned brows and tough calloused hands,
arms strong and taut from hauling bales.
The long ride home on top of the trailer,
flattened down low to dodge the low branches.
The art of stacking a rick, tying in the corners,
whilst the elevator beats out it's tireless song.
Convoys of bales marching towards the far reaches of the barn.
The satisfaction that comes as the sun goes down
on another day, knowing that the sweet precious harvest
is safely stored away from the gathering storms.
And then in the midst of a winter's blizzard,
with the snow stinging your hands and face,
You cut the strings and liberate a summer's promise.
The fragrant sweet scent of a hot July,
spilling out into the frozen feeders for hungry cattle.
Warming the soul and filling the senses,
with the assurance that there will always be another spring.

I have always loved wild flowers. I delight in finding pockets of primroses in the spring, a sure sign that winter had finally past. Pretty and delicate, but hiding an immense force.

Flower power.

Moon daisies, buttercups, celandines so bright.
Anemones and lady's smock in shades of pink and white.
Bluebells in drifts carpet woodland floors,
violets and primroses, who could ask for more?

Bees bumbling noisily inside a foxgloves bell.
Hedges hung with May blossom, a strong and musky smell.
Orchids decked in purple, standing bright and bold.
Coiled green fronds of fern waiting to unfold.

Bugle and bedstraw, the bright red pimpernel.
Pink campion and heather, the delicate harebell.
Honeysuckle twined around budding hazel trees,
dog roses rich with nectar, a treat for wild bees.

The earth is stirring, the power is immense.
Through tarmac and concrete, nature is intense.
Dandelions and daisies, cow parsley and burdocks,
their tiny little seeds hold the strength to push through rocks.

We hold in our hearts the seeds we wish to sow.
It is up to us to decide which ones we want to grow.
We can help each other and grow the seeds of hope,
tend the ones who need it and show others how to cope.

We are all like acorns, we can grow up tall and strong.
We just need a little guidance to teach us right from wrong.
We all can use some sunshine, we all should feel the rain.
We must burst the shell around us and free us from our chains.

And some of us will wither and not find any light,
or we can face the sunshine and drive away the night.
Just like the tiny daisy we have the means to flower,
and we can move mountains, if we choose to use our power.

Some days it seems that anything that can go wrong will go wrong. It is very difficult on those days to remember the good bits. The precious days when you can smile and say "I did that."

Hang on.

When the cattle get out in the silage,
when the sheep are half way to town.
When you've forgot to order more diesel,
when you feel all you do is to frown.

When the digger cuts through the mains water,
and the fox kills all of your hens.
When your tractor develops a puncture,
but you need a pint with your friends.

When you skin your shin on the harrows,
when you pierce your thumb with a nail.
When you've spent all week out fencing,
and a horse has chewed through the rails.

When your wellies start filling with water,
and your socks are stuck to your feet.
When you missed the play with your daughter,
and the storm has knocked down the wheat.

Remember the feeling you get when
you let cattle out on new grass.
And you smile as you see them cavorting,
you'll know the bad times will pass.

You may sometimes want to say sod it,
lets sell up and move to the town.
But you sense that you never would do it,
you know that you're just feeling down.

The good times make all of your effort,
worth more than a barn full of gold.
And you will have shed loads of memories,
to tell grandchildren when you are old.

Watch the sun shining bright on the meadow,
the lambs skipping off down the field.
The grain in the store before winter,
then you'll know that your soul has been healed.

Being a cowman is so much more than just milking cows. It takes years to build up a herd and know each cow, but most cowmen and women would say it is the best job on the farm.

Just a dairy farmer.

Mud stuck on your fingers, straw strands in your hair.
Clothes old and tatty, the cows don't seem to care.
Early morning milkings whilst others are in bed,
and fifty noisy young calves calling to be fed.

Misty morning round ups just before the dawn.
Eyes still hardly open, mouth set in a yawn.
Steaming cows are gathered, cudding as they wait,
and if you're really lucky they'll all be by the gate.

Milk machines are started, pulsators set the pace.
Filters all connected, the first cows are in place.
Cow cake rattles downwards, tempting others in.
Gloves and aprons fitted, they're ready to begin.

Units gasping loudly waiting for warm milk.
Cups placed on the udders, their skin a soft as silk.
Milk starts gushing quickly, turning glass jars white.
Just a lowly cowman, no one else in sight.

Udders washed and ready, teats dipped at the end.
First cows out and pushing slowly round the bend.
Bulk tanks now are filling, cooling all inside.
Yards washed down and finished, units cleaned and dried.

Cows turned out for grazing, the morning work is done.
Muck washed off the wellies, left drying in the sun.
Just another milking done for precious little pay,
but great job satisfaction at the end of every day

Lambing time is one of the most hectic, heart wrenching and exhausting times of the year. It can also be the most rewarding.

Lambing.

Breech births and heads back, bottles of gel,
no one to care if you're starting to smell.
Lambing in barns in the eye of a storm,
leaving behind a snug bed that was warm.

Being so tired that you can't hardly see,
not having time to even stop for a pee.
Calling the vet when you don't know what's wrong,
wanting to weep, but you have to stay strong.

Triplets and twins who are straggly and small,
hay in the bathroom, muck in the hall.
Starting to wonder if you will ever sleep,
spending all night out watching your sheep.

Rings in your pockets to put around tails,
bringing the flock in if it's blowing a gale.
Fingers stained purple with iodine spray.
Up in the night, then working all day.

Trying your best to get orphans to suck,
crying when you seem to run out of luck.
Doing your best for all of the flock,
not having time to look at the clock.

Giving your all to provide local fresh meat.
Lovely sweet lamb for a Sunday roast treat.
It's lonely at times and the hours can be tough,
but just being a shepherd is more than enough.

Just a few notes of caution to any city girls looking to marry a farmer!

A message to city girls looking to marry a farmer.

When you marry a farmer, your life will most likely change.
It's not all sitting by agas, admiring your home on the range.
You'll find that you're sometimes quite useful for standing in a gap,
but don't learn how to master the milking, it really is a trap!
Don't dream of having a holiday, unless it pours with rain,
Between July and September, they'll be busy hauling grain.
And then there is the planting, which will take you up to November.
In fact most months are busy, these things you need to remember.
You can say goodbye to evenings sat warming by the fire.
You could be called out to a calving or collecting a tractor tyre.
You may find there's a lamb in the kitchen, that really is quite weak,
If you can't accept that they do this your future together looks bleak.
You will find that your hall is quite crowded with wellies and bits of string.
You'll get buckets of veg on your birthday, forget it if you want bling.
And when they have been out spreading good old farm yard manure,
you may find the man that you married is lacking his sexual allure.
You also need to remember you won't need stilettos and skirts,
or old George who still does the fencing will think you are trying to flirt.
He doesn't do too much already and his heart may give up the ghost,
we don't want to have to retire him, he's useful for banging in posts.
So when you marry a farmer, it's not what you see on the telly.
You'll get used to straw on your carpet and hallways that are smelly.
But if you are happy to muck in, there is no better life,
don't be the wife of a farmer, enjoy being a farmer's wife.

Some milkings go better than others and some days you could quite happily sell the lot!

The dairy farmer.

Number nineteen's got mastitis, forty she's gone lame.
When you're a dairy farmer, no day is quite the same.
Early morning round ups, with eyes still full of sleep.
It's tempting to say sod it , let's sell them and buy sheep!

Pulsators provide a rhythm to the routine job ahead.
Your feet are slowly freezing, you wished you'd stayed in bed.
Number thirty she is waiting, she likes to be the first,
if one cow beats her to it you know your day is cursed.

Units attached firmly to each warm swinging udder,
you're ticking along nicely, then there's a bang and shudder.
A freshly calved young heifer has fallen in the pit,
she's thrashing about wildly and covering you in sh*t.

Units drop off noisily, fifteen long tails lift up.
Muck is pulsing sloppily through the dropped teat cups.
The milk is turning yellow, then a messy shade of green,
but you need to get the heifer out before you start to clean.

Number three is banging hoppers to she if she can find
a few more scraps of cow cake, she won't move her behind.
And finally you've done it, they're all back in the yard,
don't tell a dairy farmer about how your day was hard.

It is so easy to get impatient when stuck behind a tractor, this poem is just for fun, but reminds us that patience really is a virtue!

Feeling mucky.

I was driving down a country lane not very long ago,
and got stuck behind a tractor that was going rather slow.
It was a lovely sunny day and I wasn't in a hurry,
but then it turned a corner and spilled a bit of slurry.
It was a little smelly of that I am quite sure,
not everyone round here likes the smell of wet manure.
A woman rushed out from her car and shook her fist in anger.
It didn't worry me a bit, I drive a clapped out banger.
The farmer did apologise, but she did want a moan.
She called the local police force on her mobile phone.
She told them she was furious, her car was in a mess,
and if they didn't come out she'd phone the local press.
The farmer said he'd fix it if she followed him back home,
he'd use his pressure washer and a bucket full of foam.
So she drove behind the tractor until they reached the yard.
The cows were in for milking, so she found the parking hard.
She tottered on behind him in her smart stiletto heels,
he picked up the yard brush and started scraping off the wheels.
And when he had quite finished and her car was gleaming bright,
she looked in her rear mirror and gave herself a fright.
Because she was now quite covered in tiny flecks of poo.
The farmer said "I'm sorry, but my cows won't use the loo.
Please try and understand that when you work on farms

you have to shift the muck around, it won't do you any harm.
Next time perhaps you'll hang back and just admire the view,
and know that driving tractors is something we have to do".
She muttered she would try that and drove back down the road,
and swept up the long driveway to her lovely smart abode.
She told her doting husband that she was feeling rather mucky,
and he just said "How wonderful! I am so very lucky"!

My first pony was a 13.2hh skewbald. I loved that pony with all my heart, even when he got out and trampled my Mother's garden!

My pony.

Learning to ride before you can walk,
trotting in circles before you can talk.
dreaming of winning a big red rosette,
those are the days you will never forget.

The feel of the leather on well oiled soft tack,
your first time alone out on a short hack.
Your very first pony, the joy that they give,
will stay with you forever, as long as you live.

Show jumps made out of old crates and bales,
grooming and pulling rough manes and tails.
Hours spent day dreaming of winning a cup,
hitting the ground when the girths not done up.

Birthday money used to buy more bags of feed,
standing in stirrups until they have peed.
Losing control in wide open spaces,
splashing through streams with mud on bright faces.

Branches of elder to ward off the flies.
Trotting up hills under summer's blue skies.
Having a rest under leafy green trees,
grass stains on elbows, bottoms and knees.

Winning a prize in the walk trot and run.
Summer gymkhanas, a day full of fun.
Riding back home with a smile on your face,
memories you made that you'll never replace.

And you'll always remember whatever you do,
that scruffy old pony, the joy that you knew.
You may have many others but the first is the best,
if you had a small pony then you really were blessed.

I have always been a tomboy and I have the greatest respect for ladies who always look immaculate. I am even more impressed by the farm girls who have got the knack of always looking good regardless of what they have been doing!

Other women.

Other women they seem to be
on a different planet to me.
They paint their nails and dye their hair,
they always have new clothes to wear.

They go out shopping, buy flash shoes.
They like to share their fashion news.
They always look like they have spent,
more on make up than my rent.

They totter by on shoes so high,
browsing for new things to buy.
They weave their brows and shave their bits,
buy push up bras to enhance tits.

They go to spas and soak in tubs,
hire masseurs to give them rubs.
have bras that always match their knickers,
that's the life for city slickers.

They don't know what it's like to be
stuck in a patch of thick slurry.
They haven't had to calve a cow,
or lamb a ewe, they don't know how.

What would they do if they were me
and had to wee behind a tree,
or had a cow poo on their head,
I think they'd rather die instead.

I couldn't cope with all their fuss,
I think they'd frown at girls like us.
With broken nails and ingrained hands,
a sign of those who work the land.

But I don't care I wouldn't swap,
I'm not the type who likes to shop.
On a good day my hair is brushed,
I'll wash my boots if I'm not rushed.

The cows don't care about my clothes,
If I've got muck upon my nose.
I'm country born, it's in my blood,
with wellies on out in the mud.

I do not need the latest dress,
I'm used to getting in a mess.
I love my life, I hate the city,
so please don't stare at me with pity!

I love a good agricultural show, especially the smaller local shows that have retained their roots in the local community.

The local Agricultural show.

Every year in August
we have our annual show.
Cattle groomed and ready
row upon glorious row.

Stalls sprout up like magic,
food tents full to burst.
Stockmen all are hoping
that they will come in first.

Sheep are trimmed and carded,
farm names on display.
Goats there happy munching
on sweetly smelling hay.

Bands announce the opening,
trumpets fill the air.
Mums queue up for ice creams,
whilst Granny bags a chair.

A grand display of tractors,
shining in the sun.
A fairground packed with children,
having so much fun.

The craft tent is enormous,
there is so much to admire.
Carefully carved fruit bowls,
strange knitted wool attire.

There are stands for double glazing
handing out balloons.
Then noisy barrel organs,
churn out well known tunes.

Reps' are selling balers,
chicken food and tractors.
But everyone is watching
the guy who won X factor.

Chickens gaze from cages,
waiting for the judge.
Sweet stalls sell out quickly
of sticky home made fudge.

Men with bulging muscles
cut trees up with an axe.
Fast as any chainsaw
are the mighty lumberjacks.

Horses in bright harness
parade around the ring,
pulling stately coaches
once used by an old king.

Young farmers are stock judging
in freshly ironed white coats.
checking pens of cattle,
writing lots of notes.

Bales of straw for sitting on
whilst you eat your lunch.
Hog roast or a burger?
There's lots to choose to munch.

But the worst part is the toilets
the dreaded portaloo,
they don't seem very stable
and there always is a queue.

And so it all is over,
rosettes and cups presented.
Cars fill up with children
car parks slowly emptied.

It is a great occasion
where we can meet old friends,
and we hope this old tradition
will never have an end.

Farming can be very unpredictable, and when you are dealing with large animals taken off their home patch, well anything can happen!

The show champion.

A heifer has gone AWOL
from the grand arena.
they called out on the tannoy;
"Has anybody seen her"?

She started out sedately,
with polished hooves and collar.
No one had even noticed,
until they heard a holler.

She bolted from the show ring
with her handler dragged behind.
Everyone was laughing,
although it wasn't very kind.

She tipped a rustic table
where a man was selling wraps,
she was picking up momentum
and did two or three more laps.

She then got quite distracted
by a handsome Friesian bull.
He snorted from his marquee,
she was fresh and beautiful.

His top lip started curling
and he sniffed the air with lust.
She trotted up beside him
and he gave a mighty thrust.

But he was tethered firmly
to the railing in his stall,
and he missed and slipping sideways
he could only hit the wall.

She stopped to eat a hay bale
right by an ice cream stand,
where a stranger saw her munching
and he extended out his hand.

He bravely seized the moment
to grab hold of her halter,
but when he saw the size of her
he stopped and had a falter.

So she took off without him
with her tail up in the air.
Everyone was watching
but she didn't have a care.

Her owner cursing wildly
with muddied knees and coat,
crept up right behind her
and threw a rope around throat.

She didn't win the battle
but next show she won a prize;
champion beefsteak burgers
served with onions and fries!

Some days you wonder why you get out of bed! These are a few of my experiences of working on farms!

The things we do...

Chasing mad heifers who've escaped from the yard.
Using old balers that don't have a guard.
Getting cows stuck when we drop in round bales,
students who work not much faster than snails.

Arms in cows bottoms right up to our pit,
dogs on the quad bike that cover us in spit.
Trying to sleep when it's blowing a gale,
standing too still when a cow lifts her tail.

Tipping a trailer on uneven ground,
rescuing sheep that nearly were drowned.
Spreading the slurry too near to a road,
losing your bales off a unsecured load.

Having a cow fall down in the pit,
milking a heifer who's got a sore tit.
Tyres that burst when you're far from home,
ramblers demanding their freedom to roam.

Combines that break on the very last run,
lunches that melt when left out in the sun.
Bulls that decide to go down in the crush,
hitting your face when you trip on a brush.

Calves that refuse when you want them to suck,
you have to be patient, but sometimes it's luck.
Horses that shy at a bag in the ditch,
dryers that die when you flick on the switch.

Forgetting to put the plug in the bulk tank,
crossing a stream with a string and a plank.
Just a day in the life to bring your daily bread
Thank heavens for farmers who keep us all fed.

Most of us do at least some of our food shopping in supermarkets. It doesn't hurt once in a while to reflect on all the work that goes into keeping the shelves fully stocked.

Salt of the earth.

Thanks to all the people who work upon the land.
The early morning milkers, the ones who lend a hand.
The stockmen and the women who work so hard each day.
The ones who drive the tractors, lets think of them today.

The cowman with the heifer who won't come in the yard.
The shepherds out there lambing, their lives are pretty hard.
The pig man moving feeders in the pouring rain,
the contractors and the ploughmen on huge expansive plains.

The guys who rear the poultry and those who sort the eggs.
The folk who work the vineyards filling up vast kegs.
The students roguing barley and wheat up on the fens,
the sunrise and the sunset on days that never end.

Gangs of potato pickers, bringing in the crops.
The work it is relentless, to stock up all the shops.
Thanks to all the farmers, the guardians of our earth,
next time you get your shopping, remember what they're worth.

I didn't have to look far to get inspiration for this poem!

The tractor driver.

He always smells of diesel,
He has dirt under his nails.
Grease stains on his overalls,
straw when handling bales.

Oil dripped on the carpet,
mud on socks and boots.
Rags stuffed into pockets,
he's never in a suit.

Scratches on his fingers,
stains on all his clothes.
Penknife in his pocket,
chilblains on his toes.

Sleeves rolled up to elbows,
scars from welding tin.
String around his trousers,
ruddy weathered skin.

Parts of old machinery,
abandoned in the sink.
His dirty coats and wellies,
making hallways stink.

He'd never make a banker,
in pin striped suit all neat.
With briefcase full of bank notes,
clean shoes upon his feet.

He is a tractor driver,
he loves to be outside.
Ploughing up the stubble,
he takes all in his stride.

So if you get impatient
behind him driving slow,
it might just be my husband,
so wave and shout "Hello"!

This poem is for those who dream of becoming a farmer. These are just a few of the things you may come across! If you are a farmer, tick off the ones that have happened to you!

So you want to be a farmer?

Can you mend a baler as it's about to rain?
If you get knocked down by a heifer
can you work on through the pain?
Can you rescue sheep from a quagmire
up to your waist in mud,
then you cut your hand on a pen knife
and not worry about the blood?
Do you mind when you need the toilet
you have to use the nearest tree?
Do you know how to hot wire a tractor
when you've lost the only key?
Can you spot a sheep with fly strike
from the other side of a hill,
can you pretend that you are patient
when someone has broken the drill?
Can you teach a calf to drink milk
when others have given up?
Can you spot the signs of mastitis
before you put on the cups?
Do you find yourself just smiling
when you see a new born calf,
can you turn a bad experience
into a chance for a laugh?
Can you head off a bunch of cattle

who are trying to escape,
could you drive the combine harvester
without knocking down the gates?
Could you spot a sheep with footrot
before it got too lame,
or set fire to a pile of old rubbish
and not get caught in the flames?
Can you throw up tyres on the silage
as you sheet down the pit?
You may not always realise,
but you have to be pretty fit.
Would you use a bit of udder cream
to moisturise your hands,
had a quick flask of coffee
then castrate and tail lambs?
Would you rush to pick the kids up
and realise you're covered in sh*t,
and seen the looks from the others
but not worry one little bit?
Are your pockets full of washers
and odd little bits of twine?
Have you greased up the old mower
and prayed that the sun will shine?
Are you able to keep going
when everyone else is in bed?
If you can't keep up the work load,
you should try something else instead.
The thing that keeps us going

is not just a lovely view,
it's knowing each day is bringing
the chance of something new.
And sometimes we get frustrated
when things don't go to plan,
like when you need some more wormer
and your husband's gone off in the van.
It takes a special person
to cope with all the stress.
Someone who copes with pressure,
the weather and the mess.
So if you think that farming
is really the life for you,
I hope that you will read this
to see what you might have to do.
If you can get up in the morning
before the early lark,
and take the bad with the good times
then it'll be a walk in the park!

Farming has a way of getting indoors, with odd bits of machinery and straw covered overalls abandoned in the kitchen. Not everyone works outside. It can be quite challenging for those doing the cooking, cleaning and often working part time as well to keep sane at times!

Behind every Great British farmer...

I've got barley awns in the kitchen,
bits of straw in my bra.
Grains of corn in the toilet
and balls of twine in the car.

The combine wheels are turning
it's all hands now on deck.
The sun is out and shining
and has burnt the back of my neck.

The sink is full of dishes
the fridge is looking bare.
The van from home delivery
turned up when we weren't there.

So it's pasta bake for dinner
with a bit of bread and cheese.
When you are tired and hungry
you're not too hard to please.

A shear bolt's gone on the baler,
so you're asked to pop into town.
Then please drop off a flask of coffee
on your way back down.

The chickens all need feeding
the sheep have broken the fence.
The washing machine has stopped working
and things are getting tense.

And now it's getting cloudy
and it looks like it might rain.
They've got a field to finish
and are struggling to stay sane.

A friend drops in for coffee
and looks at all the mess.
She clears a space at the table,
but gets grease stains on her dress.

And our neighbour sends a postcard
from their fortnight in the sun,
wishing we could be with them
and hoping we're having fun.

Meals are left to be heated
at three a.m. in the morn.
Sometimes it can be later
if they work on until dawn.

Tired and weary farmers
leaving a rim round the bath.
Socks of straw on the carpet,
boots left out on the path.

Well done to all the farmers
who give us our daily bread,
but spare a thought for the others
who keep them all well fed!

Have you ever been so busy that you haven't had time to care about the house, until you get a phone call that is!

The phone call.

The house has got so filthy that
the dog has moved outdoors.
There's cow muck on the carpet
and oil stains on the floor.

The sink is full of dishes
the washing is piled up.
You can try to make a coffee
but you might not find a cup.

The wellies are invading
and have taken o'er the porch,
amongst the heaps of overalls
a chainsaw and a torch.

The straw bits are advancing
and have made a little path,
in piles throughout the kitchen
and in a line around the bath.

There's wormer in the hallway
it's been there since last May,
because we got distracted
and started making hay.

Some needles and syringes
are nestling in a pan,
in between the cereals
the butter and some jam.

But then we get a phone call
from relations from the city,
they want to come on over
and things aren't looking pretty.

So out come piles of bin bags,
the vacuum and the bleach.
Then I hide away the clutter
in cupboards out of reach.

I'm working like a whirlwind
I'm left to my devices.
I even clean the cooker
and the cupboard full of spices.

But I've left the back door open
and the hens have walked right in.
They have scratched out all the peelings
I had left beside by the bin.

And soon I am all hoovered
there is bloo inside the loo,
the windows have been polished
to give them a better view.

I have plugged in lots of airwicks
and sprayed curtains with Febreze,
and now we smell of cow muck
with a "hint of Summer's breeze."

I think I have been clever
and I welcome them inside.
And they sit down on the sofa,
I'm full up with inward pride.

But they move a random cushion
and find the head of a dead mouse,
that the cat thought was a present
and had brought into the house.

I can still hear distant screaming
as they race back to their car,
we may not be quite perfect
but I like it just the way we are!

Clothes shopping for a posh event is right up there on my list of top hates. I know some of you love a bit of retail therapy, but I have had some bad experiences, as this poem will tell!

I've got to buy a dress.

It's hard to go clothes shopping
when you live in wellies and jeans.
It's those or pink pyjamas
there's not much in between.

I tend to get my work clothes
from the local agri' store,
but they are sadly lacking
if you need a little bit more.

I got some decent trousers
in the Marks and Spencer sale,
and a blouse that's quite eye catching
off their bargain basement rail.

But I have been invited
to a wedding in the spring,
and I need to get an outfit
and some classy looking bling.

The first shop that I go in
has a pretty flowery dress,
but I feel like Edna Everage
and I'm getting in a stress.

The assistant tries to help me
and insists I try some on,
whilst I'm stood there in my knickers
with the creosote stains on.

I get a lacy number
stuck tight around my arms,
the curse of country living
the arms of those who farm.

It's getting quite depressing
and I'm running out of time.
I'm squashed in a pink two piece,
and she tells me I look divine.

But I see myself in the mirror
and I look like a landrace sow.
I don't have the heart to tell her,
and all I can say is "wow"!

So I wriggle out of the pig suit
and hang it back on the rail,
but she corners me by the counter
and I stifle a heartfelt wail.

This time she's found her trump card,
she holds it up with glee.
She says it is so perfect,
for someone just like me.

I see the satin ribbons,
I take in the yards of lace.
She stands there so triumphant,
a smile across her face.

I feel like Annie Oakley
crossed with an ugly sister,
she scampers round me proudly
her voice hushed to a whisper.

"Oh madam you look perfect,
that dress is so attractive."
(But the colour is bright yellow
and I feel radioactive).

This time I make a run for it
and escape out through the door,
before the dear assistant
can find me any more.

I think that I will give up
and have a look online,
then return to jeans and sweatshirts
and a bottle full of wine!

Harvest time is very special. The whole arable year has been planned around getting maximum yields. Once the wheels start turning and the weather settles there is seldom any let up until the job is done.

Harvest.

I can hear the combine humming
far into the night.
Tractors lined up waiting,
fields are full of lights.

Harvest has now started,
a race against the rain.
Filling up big trailers
with heaps of golden grain.

Tired and dusty farmers
with pockets full of straw,
piling up the driers
filling up the store.

Dinners left to microwave,
family life on hold.
Every waking minute
spent working fields of gold.

All the world is busy
enjoying days of sun,
but tractor wheels keep turning
once the harvest has begun.

I wanted to end this little collection of rhymes with a nod to our ancestors. I think they would be astounded by modern farming techniques, but I think most of us still have the same goals and aspirations of those gone before us.

The golden years.

The little farms with just one cow,
an old shire horse to pull the plough.
A few hens scratching in the yard,
back in the day work was so hard.

A pig to fatten for the pot,
but folk were happy with their lot.
A cow to milk with pail and stool,
before the banks and shops would rule.

A scythe to cut the meadow grass,
a kettle made of polished brass.
A candle burning through the night,
to give a tiny guiding light.

The veg' preserved with salty brine,
the buckets full of homemade wine.
Sweet jams and chutneys in thick jars,
no people rushing by in cars.

A blackened grate that warmed the heart,
veg' loaded on the horse and cart.
The village folk helped haul the corn,
the golden days before we were born.

Those times are gone, little remains,
the ricks of hay, the grassy lanes.
The horses now replaced with tractors,
the massive kit owned by contractors.

But underneath we're just the same,
the little spark is now a flame.
They may have gone, those folk of old,
but we have learned from what they told.

The land is now for us to tend,
the farmer's lot will never end.
The whispers of their stories live,
in all we do and all we give.

Lightning Source UK Ltd.
Milton Keynes UK
UKOW06f1323040917
308553UK00008BA/92/P